My Guinea Pigs

A Fill-in-the-Blank Photo and Memory Book

**The Book for Your Guinea Pigs!
Fill in, Glue, and Design!**

A house without animals

is like a sky

without stars.

Profile - Guinea Pig Owner

[Photo]

_____

Name: _____

Date of birth: _____

Zodiac sign: _____

Interests: _____
_____

Favorite animal: _____

Favorite color: _____

Photo

_____

Why I like guinea pigs:

_____

_____

The following guinea pigs are a part of my life:

_____

_____

_____

Guinea Pig - Profile #1

[Photo]

My full name is ...	
Most of the time, my owner calls me ...	
My birthday is on ...	
My zodiac sign is ...	
My gender is ...	
My exact breed is ...	
The color of my fur is ...	
My favorite pastime is ...	

I can be described as:

☐ *social*   ☐ *shy*
☐ *brave*   ☐ *anxious*
☐ *dominant*   ☐ *cautious*
☐ *curious*   ☐ *cuddly*
☐ *playful*   ☐ *affectionate*
☐ *high-spirited*   ☐ *timid*
☐ *wild*   ☐ *reserved*
☐ *trusting / someone to confide in*   ☐ *cozy*
☐ _____
☐ _____

This is what I love to eat the most:

☐ *Fresh hay*   ☐ *Dandelions*
☐ *Grass*   ☐ *Picked herbs*
☐ *Vegetables*   ☐ *Small branches and twigs*
☐ *Fruits*
☐ _____
☐ _____

Guinea Pig - Profile #2

[Photo]

My full name is ...	
Most of the time, my owner calls me ...	
My birthday is on ...	
My zodiac sign is ...	
My gender is ...	
My exact breed is ...	
The color of my fur is ...	
My favorite pastime is ...	

I can be described as:

☐ social
☐ brave
☐ dominant
☐ curious
☐ playful
☐ high-spirited
☐ wild
☐ trusting / someone to confide in
☐ _____
☐ _____

☐ shy
☐ anxious
☐ cautious
☐ cuddly
☐ affectionate
☐ timid
☐ reserved
☐ cozy

This is what I love to eat the most:

☐ Fresh hay
☐ Grass
☐ Vegetables
☐ Fruits
☐ _____
☐ _____

☐ Dandelions
☐ Picked herbs
☐ Small branches and twigs

Guinea Pig - Profile #3

Photo

_____

My full name is ...	
Most of the time, my owner calls me ...	
My birthday is on ...	
My zodiac sign is ...	
My gender is ...	
My exact breed is ...	
The color of my fur is ...	
My favorite pastime is ...	

I can be described as:

- ☐ social
- ☐ brave
- ☐ dominant
- ☐ curious
- ☐ playful
- ☐ high-spirited
- ☐ wild
- ☐ trusting / someone to confide in
- ☐ _____
- ☐ _____

- ☐ shy
- ☐ anxious
- ☐ cautious
- ☐ cuddly
- ☐ affectionate
- ☐ timid
- ☐ reserved
- ☐ cozy

This is what I love to eat the most:

- ☐ Fresh hay
- ☐ Grass
- ☐ Vegetables
- ☐ Fruits
- ☐ _____
- ☐ _____

- ☐ Dandelions
- ☐ Picked herbs
- ☐ Small branches and twigs

Where We Were Picked Up

_____
_____
_____
_____
_____

[Photo]

_____
_____

Our Parents

Photo

Photo

Our Siblings

[Photo]

[Photo]

Photo

Photo

We as Babies

[Photo]

_____

[Photo]

Photo

Photo

Photo

_____

Photo

First Day in Our New Home

This is the day we moved in:

_____

The first thing we did there was:

_____

Our behavior at that time was:

_____

Photo

_____

Photo

Photo

This is Our Territory

That belongs to our home:

- ☐ *Our cage*
- ☐ *Outdoor hutch*
- ☐ *Grass house*
- ☐ *Comfortable bed*
- ☐ *Cozy cuddle cave*
- ☐ *Grass Tunnel*
- ☐ *Wooden ladder*
- ☐ *Toilet box*
- ☐ *Hay rack*
- ☐ *Our food bowl*
- ☐ *Water bottle*
- ☐ *Feed balls / Play balls*
- ☐ *And also:*

_____

_____

_____

_____

Photo

Our Home

[Photo]

[Photo]

Photo

Photo

We Like it Here

Photo

Photo

Photo

Photo

Sleep and Dream

These are our favorite places to sleep:

_____

_____

_____

_____

| Photo |

We Love to Play

These are our favorite toys:

_____

_____

_____

_____

_____

Photo

Feeding Time

Grass, hay, herbs and fruits,

makes every guinea pig happy!

_____

_____

Photo

Photo

_____

Photo

Photo

_____

Photo

Photo

Photo

Guinea Pigs Are Very Clean Animals

Photo

Photo

Photo

Photo

We Don´t Like Vets

We Play and Have Fun

Photo

_____

Photo

We Run and Jump

Photo

Photo

Photo

Photo

We Enjoy Our Life

Photo

Photo

Photo
Photo

Here We Are with Our Owner

_____
_____
_____
_____
_____
_____

Photo

Photo

_____

Photo

Photo

Photo

Our Summer House

In summer we like to be outside in nature.

_____
_____

Photo

We Love to Be Outside

Photo

Photo

Friendships with Other Animals

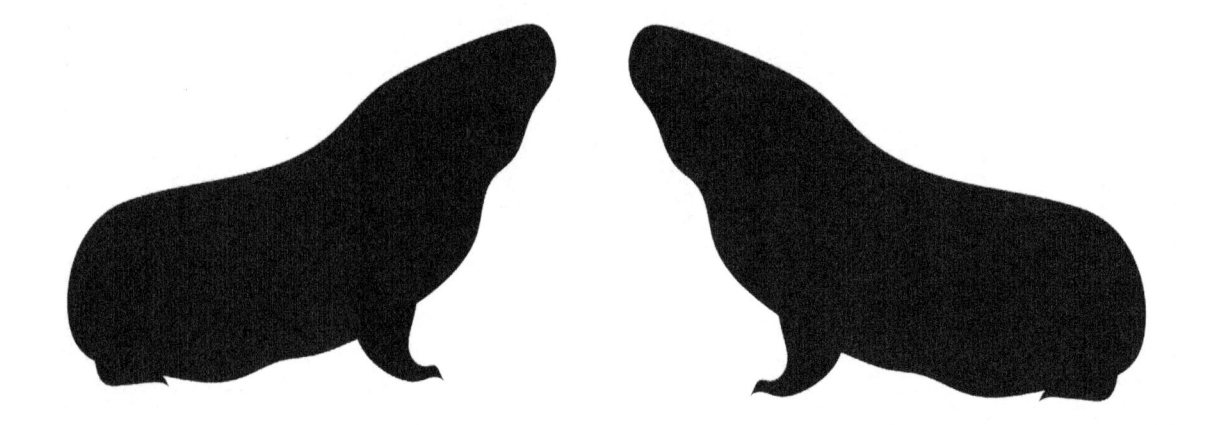

_____

_____

| Photo |

Photo

Photo

Photo

Photo

We Explore the World

Photo

Photo

Photo

Photo

Guinea Pigs - Adventures

Photo

Photo

Photo

Photo

Photo

Photo

Photo

Here Are Some of the Best Photos of Us

Photo

Photo

Photo

Photo

Photo

Photo

Photo

Comments and Notes:

My Pets

*A Fill-in-the-Blank Book
and Photo Album*

My Pets
**A Fill-in-the-Blank Book
and Photo Album
ISBN: 9798582433927**

Do you have a horse and two dogs?
Or maybe your home is filled with cats?
Perhaps you have two rabbits for the kids?

For this album, it doesn't matter —
here, there's enough space to capture
all of the special moments and memories you've shared with your pets.

This book contains space for 6 pets,
regardless of whether the pet is a dog, cat, or mouse.
20 pages are dedicated to each animal;
these pages include space for a detailed profile, photos, and special moments.
With this book, build a token of remembrance
for all the wonderful pets you've shared your home with!

Only available on Amazon!

My Rabbits
ISBN 9798586943620
With profiles for 3 rabbits
and space for 150 photos!

My Guinea Pigs
ISBN 9798587208155
With profiles for 3 guinea pigs
and space for 150 photos!

My Chinchillas
ISBN 9798587210448
With profiles for 3 chinchillas
and space for 150 photos!

Photo and Memory Album for Your Pets!

Gift your loved ones a lifelong memory.
Equipped with profiles for several animals and plenty of space for your favorite photos, this album makes the perfect present.

Here, you have the opportunity to categorically record and preserve everything about your beloved companions.
Their favorite place to sleep, how they played and had fun, the walks you shared…
And, of course, all of the wonderful photos with their owner.

Write down the most important information and characteristics in each animal profile and create a memorable album — built with handy fill-in-the-blanks!

Available for rabbits, guinea pigs and chinchillas.

Only available on Amazon!

Copyright © Christine Schmitt 2020 1st Edition

*All rights reserved.
Reproduction, full or partial, is not permitted.
No part of this work may be reproduced, duplicated, or distributed in any form
without written permission from the author.
Any violations will be prosecuted.*

*Based on the original book:
Meine Meerschweinchen - Ein Foto- und Erinnerungsalbum; Christine Schmitt 2020 1st Edition*

Contact: Christine Schmitt / Kreuzhofstr. 7a / 93083 Obertraubling / Germany
Email: crisy63@hotmail.com

Cover Design: Christine Schmitt
Cover Photo: © Picture Partners / www.shutterstock.com
Interior Graphics: © Airin.dizain / www.shutterstock.com
Backcover Photo: © Sascha Preussner / www.shutterstock.com

ISBN 9798587208155

Printed in Great Britain
by Amazon